HOMING

JOHN MOLE

Homing

SECKER & WARBURG
LONDON

First published in England 1987 by
Martin Secker & Warburg Limited
54 Poland Street, London W1V 3DF

Copyright © John Mole 1987

British Library Cataloguing in Publication Data

Mole, John, 1941–
Homing.
I. Title
821'.914   PR6063.O483

ISBN 0–436–28041–8

Typeset by Inforum Ltd, Portsmouth
Printed in England by
Redwood Burn Ltd, Trowbridge

for MARY

ACKNOWLEDGEMENTS

Some of these poems have appeared, previously, in the following publications: *Argo, Cambridge Review, Country Life, Encounter, London Magazine, New Statesman, New Yorick, Oxford Magazine, Poetry Review, South West Review, Times Literary Supplement, Words.*

'An Amateur Water-colourist to Thomas Girtin' was first published in *With a Poet's Eye* (Tate Gallery, 1986).

Extracts from 'From Doctor Watson's Casebook' have been broadcast on *Poetry Now* (BBC Radio 3).

'The Song of the Pie', 'A Short History of State Funerals', 'Learning the Ropes' and 'Home' have appeared in a limited edition from the Gruffy-ground Press (1986).

'Moth' originally appeared as a verse riddle in *Once There Were Dragons* by John Mole and Mary Norman (André Deutsch, 1979).

CONTENTS

ADDER

Walking my own blue hills,
The Quantocks,
I disturb an adder
And remember –

Victory V,
Black V for venom,
Churchill's long cigar,
The hiss of Hitler,

Tongue-flick
In the crackling undergrowth
Of intermittent
Wireless wavebands,

Vy the viper
Couldn't vipe her . . .
Even our riddles
Had a German accent.

Snake in the grass
But not our garden
Where no handkerchief
Would wave surrender,

Herr Leviathan,
The Poisonous One,
Monster of coils
And vivid markings . . .

In my dream, inside
A Chilprufe sleeping suit,
I killed him nightly
With bare hands.

COMING HOME

The son they love came home then went away.
They asked him why he cried out every night.
He didn't tell them and he couldn't stay.
They try to reach him but he'll never write.
They lie together now. They sleep apart
And still, in dreams, each breaks the other's heart.

And still, in dreams, he's haunted by a child
That stood a moment, looked into his eyes
Not guessing just how far he was defiled,
As if his combat-jacket were disguise.
Don't let the little bastards get to you.
You know exactly what you have to do.

All wars are guilty of their own remorse
And have it out with us before they end.
Some may be just, no doubt. Of course.
In time your enemy becomes your friend.
But there are debts the future can't reclaim –
To kill a child and not to know its name.

To kill a child that couldn't run away,
That stood a moment after it was shot
With puzzled human eyes as if to say
Like you I was so why now am I not?
Then fell. He shot the mother too.
It seemed exactly what he had to do.

And then it seemed exactly where to be
Was nowhere where he had to think of home,
The horror of all words meant lovingly,
The ignorant kindness everyone had shown.
Not only nightmares slay the innocent
And that's the reason why he came and went.

And that's the reason why this can't go on,
And why it's almost culpable to write,
And why I can't stop thinking of our son
And of how easily we sleep at night,
How in this house if anybody screams
We joke next morning. It was only dreams.

Oh only dreams that simply come and go,
That tell us nothing that we can't forget.
We lie beside each other snugly, two
Such comfortable, cautious parents, yet
There was a child who came and went away.
They said *We love you* but he could not stay.

FIRSTLINGS

for Simon and Ben

First Snow

Whose is this long, unexpected elbow
Resting its white sleeve on the wall?
Is anyone out there when I call
To hear my voice? I've lost my echo.

Whose are those feathery tears that keep coming?
Somebody weeps without a sound
And leaves his grief heaped up on the ground.
It's so quiet my ears are drumming.

Whose is that handkerchief on the gatepost
Large enough for a giant sneeze?
Bless you whisper the shivering trees
While I just stand here like a ghost.

Who am I? And where have I woken?
It wasn't the same when I went to bed.
I still feel me inside my head
Though now a different language is spoken.

Suddenly all the meanings have gone.
Is someone trying to tell me something?
A bird shakes silver dust from its wing
And the sky goes on and on and on.

Moth

Pity my silence pressing at your window
Frail and motionless against the night;
A baffled spectre framed by blackness,
Little moonflake, prisoner of glass.
This is my journey's end, receive me.
Brilliant keeper, rise and let me in.

Then later, when from a drawer perhaps
You take my body, wasted, brittle
As a shred of antique parchment, hold it
Gently up to the light I loved
But which bewildered me, until
I fly away again, a ghostly powder
Blown or shaken from your hand.

The Lost Boy

Mother, oh mother,
Your cupboard's not bare.
I know without looking
The lost boy's in there.

His bones are all shiny.
He's wearing my shoes.
It wasn't his picture
They showed on the News.

Our telephone's ringing.
Why do you just sit
Like a difficult puzzle
The last piece won't fit?

And where is my father?
What have you both done?
Will somebody find me?
Is the lost boy your son?

His footprints are my prints.
There's blood on the floor.
Oh mother, dear mother,
Let me open the door.

The Trick

One night, when I couldn't sleep,
My Dad said
Think of the tomatoes in the greenhouse

And I did.
It wasn't the same as counting sheep
Or anything like that.

It was just not being in my room forever
On a hot bed
Restless, turning and turning,

But out there, with the patient gaze of moonlight
Blessing each ripe skin
And our old zinc watering-can with its sprinkler,

Shining through a clear glass pane
Which slowly clouded over into
Drowsy, comfortable darkness

Till I woke and came downstairs to breakfast
Saying *Thank you, Dad,*
I thought of them. It did the trick.

HOME

They've called it *Remember* –
Near the front gate
A bijou bi-plane spins its propeller
Pipping each post – phut phut –

While its hinged mannikin
Never short of wind
Cranks and cranks the handle
Over, down, and

Up, then breezily over
In endless recall
Which goes on turning forever
Like nothing at all.

LEARNING THE ROPES

Dear Doctor Universe,
Your medicine ball
Is our dream bolus,
A coveted cure-all:
These are the ropes
And we are learning them.

Brisk mats bristle
As expertise should
But you blow your whistle –
No bloody good!
These are the ropes
And we are learning them.

The floor shines so.
It reflects your skill,
The cold walls echo
Overkill Overkill –
These are the ropes
And we are learning them.

That high wooden horse
Where you somersault
Resembles a hearse –
It is not your fault.
These are the ropes
And we are learning them.

Parallel bars
Mount, rung by rung,
To extravagant stars
Where your praise is sung:
These are the ropes
And we are learning them.

All your equipment
Is in its place –
Oh betterment, betterment
By disgrace:
These are the ropes
And we are learning them.

Dear Doctor Universe,
Let us pay
For our just deserts
With an apple a day:
These are the ropes
And we are learning them.

JUDGEMENTAL ATTITUDES

They lived in exquisite misery
For others' betterment.
They died
With *It's not for us to say* upon their lips.

We never thanked them
To their satisfaction.
It was their satisfaction
That we never did.

A rinsed transmogrification of hair-dos
Into the empyrean,
They gave each doom-dark cloud
Its silver lining.

SMOKE RINGS

Once more, this stubborn ghost
Shines briskly at me
Through his smoke rings
Like an indoor firework
Sparkling on the hearth.

My fiscal deity,
A little Caesar
Wreathed in recurrent
Clouds of knowing
Where the pennies come from.

What have I rendered him
But random poems
He has not approved of –
Innocent investments
Never adding up.

Oh talent, profitless return –
To put just one word
Where his mouth is,
Calling my children home
To light the big cigar.

Now he would say
We understand each other.
In this world of real transaction
There is only duty
Which must still be paid.

But, unappeased again,
He puffs a last contemptuous ring
Around my fingers
As they add this column
To another page.

THE SONG OF THE PIE

It is time to bake our pie.
   The brave beaks clack together,
But look at each beady eye
   As it reckons the price of a feather.

The brave beaks clack together:
   Our recipe must be the best
As it reckons the price of a feather
   And takes good care of your nest.

Our recipe must be the best.
   It offers you dozens of eggs
And takes good care of your nest
   If you stand on your own thin legs.

It offers you dozens of eggs.
   There's a special way to take them.
If you stand on your own thin legs
   You are much less likely to break them.

There's a special way to take them
   That you'll know if you've used eggs before.
You are much less likely to break them
   When you have a few thousand in store.

That you'll know if you've used eggs before
   Is our a priori assumption.
When you have a few thousand in store
   You deserve some reward for gumption.

Is our a priori assumption
   Unreasonable, do you think?
You deserve some reward for gumption.
   Only the bad eggs stink.

Unreasonable, do you think?
   But why should you make such a fuss?
Only the bad eggs stink.
   All the best eggs vote for us.

But why should you make such a fuss
  When we promise that things will go well?
All the best eggs vote for us.
  They know it's the truth we tell.

When they promise that things will go well
  It is time to bake their pie.
We know it's the truth they tell,
  But look at each beady eye.

MORWENSTOW

'I would not be forgotten in this land'
                                    R.S. Hawker

Golden commerce
With an insect city
Stalking its colonnades
Of coastal barley.

Be wise, sluggard,
Look to the ant,
The ladybird, the Meadow Brown –
Awake! Awake!
                *
Or the bees' prudence
In a high wind:
Each of them picks a pebble up
For steady flight –

Thus Robert Hawker
Teasing Thomas Acland –
Then he drops it, sir,
At the hive's entrance.
                *
Too many names now
Crowd the shivered timbers.
Parson Kilroy
You were here and here,

This boxed scriptorium
Your hut of samples –
Not all epitaphs
Are writ on water.
                *
Bless the breakers
In the name of all those broken
As our cry comes unto thee
Mon Père! Mon Père!

How shall we know
Our God made manifest?
No fog, no wind, no rain,
No congregation.

*

Orient but mortal
Stepping west,
An opiate blossom
Amongst ripened corn.

Across the sea
A crimson sunset
Sheds its petals
One by one.

*

Come to thy God in time,
Thy Lord at last:
Remote, unfriended,
Melancholy, slow.

A very awful path
The final journey
Though the burden of this parish
Was a crucial pain.

*

Catholic, Anglican,
What matter
At the last withdrawing roar
From bone, granite,

To the gold horizon,
To a hive of air
Where every soul comes home
And drops its ballast.

JOHN WESLEY PREACHING AT GWENNAP PIT

Here at this depth I am stunned by faith,
Its visitation a small stone dislodged
From the Lord's mountain – that sheer ledge –
Come whispering at first like scree
Then gathered to the resonance of wrath
And veritable hugeness hurled at me.

What else beside the multitudes, my God?
Their hallelujahs, their pale smitten faces
Marvellously thralled, the tumbling innocence of grace
That rolls and roars so playfully to heaven –
Oh strict seizure, madness in my method,
I am all tongues and one thing to all men.

THE GIFT

So, if it seems
That only
Nowhere's left
Then go there
Willingly.

Let now
Slip through your fingers
Like dry earth,
Let soon
Be your rain-dance.

Between here
And there
The clouds are blossoming.
They wave
On stems of sunlight.

Gather them
Unthinking
In a loving armful
As their gilded burden
Welcomes your return.

Then, though it seem
That only
Nowhere's left
You'll stay here
Willingly.

LIVING WITH MOTHER

Already at the door, her
Fearsome hyper-greeting
Grabs their arrival: *Lovely, so*
You're here, you're home, so
Lovely. We've been waiting
Ever since you rang, and when you didn't . . .
We were worried, Mum and I, and . . .
All of you, at last, so lovely,
Let me . . .
     Then it's
All of them packed round
The kitchen table's awkward cosiness
For ceremonial rock-buns,
Ginger cake and *I'll be Mother*
Till she comes. She's upstairs resting. How
This poor house rattles when you've gone
With just the two of us, but lovely
Now with all of us again . . .
And for the kids she's written
WELCOME HAPPY DAYS
And TOTTENHAM OK
In red magnetic letters
On the fridge.

ANSWER PHONE

Please leave your name.
I shall call you back.
There is no one here.
Do you have a number?

Do you have a cat?
I have four children.
They keep me busy.
They should be back.

I shall call your number.
My mind is empty.
There is no one there.
Please leave my name.

Please leave my cat.
He has no number.
Do you want four children?
They have names.

Please name your children.
My cat is Rover.
He will call you back.
I keep him busy.

THE DOLL'S HOUSE

We are not speaking.
I have taken your words
And you mine.
They miss each other
Like homesick children.

I have hidden your words
In the Study:
They are *Cooker*,
Washing Machine, *Deep-freeze*
And *Do you love me?*

You have hidden my words
In the kitchen:
They are *Club*,
Appointment, *Handicap*
And *Where is my shirt?*

After tonight
We shall probably find them.
If not,
They have lived with us long enough
To find their own way back.

THE STATION WIFE

1

This is me and Anna
In our masks and combat jackets
On the runway and that's
Gas that yellow you can almost
See the edges and the men
Inside it with their hoses laughing
At how silly we looked they said
And looking just as silly I'd say
Like space-invaders in a field
Of mustard Anna says
We all look silly and we'd
All be dead if this was real
Though if we keep prepared
We won't be which is why
We're practising and anyway
It all looks real enough to me
And even Jacqueline admits
To feeling just a little sexy
Taking us with all those men
Behind us and us sort of
Crouching there like that and
Grinning underneath our masks
But what's so really good's
The definition of the edges
Round that yellow cloud
With all the men inside
And them so blurry even Jacqui's
Pleased with how this one came out.

2

This is Sue and Debbie
On the rifle range I
Took it and that's
Greg and Terry lying there
Beside them straightening
Their aim and swopping wives

Said Terry with his other arm
Round Debbie's shoulder
So what next I wondered as
The rounds of ammo thudded into
Mannikins with bullseyes
Where their parts would be
Then all of us ran up and counted
While the dummies stood there
With their eyes all dead and staring
Like a seizure and the men exclaiming
Well done girlie with their arms
Around the targets' shoulders begging
Take us take us till I laughed
So much I couldn't get it
In and nor can Trevor
Anymore says Anna but I
Wish I had so you could see
The weird resemblances there were
Between those riddled mannikins
And Greg and Terry.

3

This is Tracy standing by the wire
With cutters for a laugh you
Can't tell which side of the fence
She's on but then what happened is
The reason I can't laugh or tell you
What there is to tell since no one told us
Why the siren why the inner gates
Were closed and why our men
Ran criss-cross in the distance then
Assembled on the runway I
Could just see Trevor Greg
And Terry then a tall guard
Snatched my camera saying
Later love you'll get it back

And there's me wondering
What would I do if this was real
Or if it is this time
And where the children are
And must we stay forever with
These skulls this hardware all
The loveless sexiness of being here
Inside the wire outside
The inner gates where even Paul
Goes running criss-cross at
What secret purposes then
Comes home high to hoist his
Penis up and tell me
Baby take a photograph of that.

MESSIAEN

for Christel and Alexander Baillie

'Conceived and written in the course of my captivity, the *Quartet for the End of Time* was performed for the first time in Stalag 8-A on January 15, 1941 . . .'

Olivier Messiaen

1

Slowly, as the theme
Becomes your face,
Its agonies of grace
Appal yet seem
At rest, declare
All pain resolved
To liberty and held
On safe, immaculate air.

2

The pizzicato of a quick
Grief plucks at its bars –
Your dreams release each prisoner's
Pride from his panic.

3

The world prepares its instruments. Whoever cries
Keeps time with Time and learns to temporise.

4

After the last held note
Returns us to ourselves, we cling
To your gift, the sustaining
Promise of silence,
And we live in hope
As you did, as your innocence
Survived the cut-throat
Darkness of Europe.

24

NACHTSTÜCK

Polished fingernails on catgut –
The clean murders
Tuned to perfection and played
Without consequence.

Melodious edicts
Pitching their pain
In a glint of manicure
And all four strings.

No blood on these hands
Or even the distant
Arpeggio shrieking
Of one small child

But a sweet glissade
As the dying fall
Dissolves in silence
Washing clean –

Apotheosis
Of the guilty maestro;
No one calls him
To the least account.

There are other ways
Than the butcher's hook,
The piano wire
And the gods' home movies.

LAST NIGHT

Last night, grown children
Gathered their future in fistfulls
To hurl at each other
And a pale hand pulled
The curtains close which of all

Hands belonged to the last man
Left in the city to vote
Who shrugged, turned on
The radio and listened –
It is not safe out.

THE STRANGER

A neighbour said he'd come from Germany
But that was long ago
And many miles from here.
He seemed quite happy in our garden.

As I recall, he hummed a lot
And pottered. When he took them boating
Both the children called him Uncle
On account of his moustache.

Sad, though, the way he chewed it
So whole tufts came out, then went on humming.
I don't remember what composers now –
But a little Mozart, I think.

A SHORT HISTORY OF STATE FUNERALS

after Charles de Vion

Such a rumpus at the door,
   Such a racket of protection.
   Who would have thought death's mere defection
   Needs such a ceremonial roar.
Anyhow, they let us in –
   God knows who sent the invitation –
   Red-carpet treatment – like some station
   In Moscow or Berlin
Except that the train had left already,
   Not for London, Warsaw, Vladi-
   vostok . . . No, but the shabby
Terminal disgrace
   That time calls History
   And which wears our face.

TOY BRICKS

Take two for the man-child
Fury, to be hurled
At a helplessness marked NO
Which is all of your world
And your father's, where nothing is piled
Times nothing into which
Nothing will seem to go.

Build says mother. *Imagine yourself*
Inside it. She has papered the walls
With dinner money. *We are not rich*
Like television, but with luck and the school's
Help . . . On a high shelf
The last baked beans are a balancing trick
Above an empty fridge.

To wake one day to the wolf's
Huff and puff – his jaw
Slavering as he follows you to school.
He knows a house of straw
When he sees one. His impatient face
Is teacher's. You have a toy brick
In each pocket. This is not a good place.

This is not television. Outside,
Real people stamp their feet
Around a brazier, hugging their shoulders –
Take nothing from nothing, divide
By nothing times police and soldiers.
Jack builds his house on *Playschool*.
The wolf waits in the street.

At dinner-break your steaming mash
Has misted the glass. You draw
Two fierce eyes and the familiar jaw,
Take blatant aim and smash
The system. Shameless, you stand there
Rigid, bitter, frowning, without tears.
The splintering chime is music to your ears.

Build said mother. You have not.
She comes for you. She weeps,
Recriminates, but doesn't understand.
Something has hold of you for keeps.
You stride ahead, beyond her, as the gulf
Between you opens, as you take his hand
And walk home with the wolf.

CONDEMNED

I sat next to Dad at breakfast
And we ate a hearty meal
But his face, long as a judge's,
Stared at the family mail
As if looks could kill –

Together, we sentenced the world
To life. Our tears were wet.
Mum threw salt over her left shoulder
And put a hard-boiled egg in my pocket
To eat now that I'm older.

TRANSLATION

On this side of a wall
You place your ladder
Wondering which side of whose wall
It stands against

While on the other side
A man is talking
About this and that
To do with walls

Like whose side of the wall
Becomes the other
If you climb it first
And see his ladder

Or if each side
Offers either
Both the ladders
But no wall

Until at last
You face each other
Wondering who was who
Or why at all

Your wall or his
Required a ladder:
Hypocrite lecteur,
Je suis l'écrivain.

HOW HIGH

How High the Chinaman
Is tired of their question.
He says *I am short*
But then they ask him
How low can you get?

Ah so he says
How low is an Englishman
Is hard to answer
Nor is a joke a joke
In bad translation.

THE CONJURORS

They came and went
At my friends' parties
Always asking us to
Please be of assistance –

To peer up sleeves
And pummel bowlers,
Take a card from somewhere
Near the middle of the pack.

Their jokes were a mystique
The adults laughed at
Like a cloudy rabbit
Hung above our heads.

In stained white
Waiters' gloves, each ghostly finger
Frisked our future
With a shrimp's translucence.

Though we cheered
And cried *Hey Presto!*
All the best games started
After they had gone.

FROM DOCTOR WATSON'S CASEBOOK

The Case of What He Ordered

No, not this afternoon, Holmes, not the violin.
A good read's more the ticket, don't you think?
Not the *Police Gazette* . . . A book you could get lost in,
Foreign climes etc. What? No, not that Chink
With the fingernails – too close to home.
You really must relax. No, absolutely not,
You've read it twice already. Which? *The Moonstone?*
Gracious, old boy, be sensible. Less plot, less plot.

The Case of The Ten Green Bottles

Look, Mrs H, between you and me
And the old five-barred proverbial, as it were,
I'm sure they don't fall accidentally.
They're being pushed. Haven't you noticed since he
                    put them there
How strangely he's behaved? No, I haven't exactly seen
Him do it, but he's not like himself at all –
Ten bottles, Watson, he told me, *and they must be green.*
A normal chap hangs pictures on the wall.

The Case of The Missing Proverb

Dash it, Holmes, sometimes you go too far.
This is the wrong tree that you're barking up.
Of course you're a genius, I know you are,
But why can't you ever stop?
Two in the bush, old man? What's that?
Half the time, you know, I just can't understand
A word you say. You're talking through your hat!
One in the . . . One *what? Whose* hand?

The Case of The Apologetic Parenthesis

Yes, yes, dear reader, I make
Allowances. Life would be very dull
Without him. No, I can't have my cake
And eat it, but it's pretty awful
When you always get the crumbs *before*
They've fallen from the great man's table
If you see what I mean . . . (I'm a bad hand at metaphor)
And I'm far too agreeable.

The Case of The Amazing Coincidence

Absolutely, Holmes, oh yes, bang
On, old man, you must be right –
What else, indeed, but an orang-outang
Would have left its prints tonight
At just this spot beneath the Major's window?
Yes, I did hear that strangled cry.
Holmes, you've done it, by jingo!
Oh my! Oh my! Oh my! Oh my! Oh my!

The Case of The Remorseless Conjunction

There are times, believe me Lestrade,
When I'm jolly glad of my revolver,
Times when I tell him *Bring in Scotland Yard*
But he won't (of course), when we're knee-deep in heather
On Dartmoor (and gorse) and he hasn't a clue
And he's *loving* it and there's probably quicksand
And a bally hound with luminous fur and I mention you
In passing and he gives me that look and . . .

The Case of The Déjà Vu

Well, Holmes, another handsome lady
Called while you were out – black veil,
Something about a letter, obviously
End of her tether don't you know. Blackmail.

The usual jitters. So I sat her down
Until she'd calmed a bit, then she upped and went
Leaving her card (they all do) with an out-of-town
Address. Shall I call a cab? No, this time it's Kent.

The Case of The Fulfilled Wish

Reader, one posthumous account
And then that's that, I promise you.
I've had my bellyful. I can't
Take any more. Here's what I'm going to do:
A leaf from Moriarty's book –
I'll lure him to some dangerous high place
Then . . . *Look behind you, Holmes old fellow, look!*
And that will be our very last last case.

TWO JAZZ ELEGIES

Portrait of Pee Wee

A face so lugubrious it seemed
The very mould of
All keys minor, jalousie brow
Pulled down, and every feature
Hang-dog –

Ebony growl, a throaty
Lifeline, wind in those reeds
Each chosen for the frottage
Of sweet sandpaper,
Piper, Pee Wee –

A tone such as the heart
Might find in beating
Four to the bar then
Taking one last breath –

When, not long before you died,
You visited your wife in hospital
A nurse observed

Why, even his feet look sad.

*

Cottontail

Echo of plenty,
Cock of the sax-walk
And still lording it, a cornucopia
That poured itself away
In bitter sweet-talk
When your horn was empty,

You sat at the bar
And listened while, bright-eyed,
The jazz-buff bushy-tails
Kept asking *Say, aren't you Ben Webster?*
Until you had to answer, grim
But laconic always, *I'm what's left of him.*

Or, late for a festival,
You blew two choruses then staggered
From the bandstand moaning *Somebody call
The Doctor* and they fetched him
Straight in his tumbler
Winking an amber eye and saying

Once to have been great
Is to be greatly exhausted
At the end, but with a terminal panache
Which keeps your old flame
Kindled and still burning
Under the ash.

THE IMPERTINENCE OF THE THING

Past forty, a lyricist
Unsung, prone to self-pity
And troubled by the dead
Weight of every
Line, each further from my best,

I think of the young Joyce just
Happening to pass through London
On Yeats's birthday, or
(Was it?) expressly come
To do what must be done

When the time arrives
In all poets' lives
Which was (ie) to make straight
For the Cavendish where W.B.
Sat ensconced in state

Correcting proofs while sipping
Luke-warm jasmine tea
And not expecting anything
At all like this considering
The eminence of already distinguished *gris*

He might reasonably
Have assumed – Well, Joyce
(Says Oliver Gogarty) knocked on Yeats's door
And in readiness was
Clearing his thin voice

With bat-eyes narrowing
Behind their lenses when
Yeats, his sight already
None too good either, in that familiar sing-
Song called *Come in!*

Then turned to the young blur
Suddenly framed there
And heard *What age are you, sir?*
To which *I'm forty*
He replied, and presumably thought he'd

Appear quite grand, quite mezzo del cammin
To the young fellow who would not come in
But who explained simply
You are too old for me
To help, I bid you goodbye said he

And went, leaving W.B.
(Says Gogarty) *amazed by the impertinence*
Of the thing, but good for Joyce
Say I, sound sense,
And good for the old peacock too

Because there's nothing like a witty
Exchange between the greats
(Bravo Joyce *and* Yeats!)
To reduce a poet's dull self-pity
To absurdity

And so, being older
Than either was then,
Let me laugh now with one
Now the other
And now with both men.

This poem is based on Hugh Kenner's version of Gogarty's
anecdote which can be found in his book *A Colder Eye.*

NEW DRESSES

So many mirrors
In the Summerwear department
As I stumble past them
With a basketful
Of rice and pasta

Which should be a hamper
And my poem no less
A picnic for this solemn girl
Who comes to read
The small print of new dresses

Pressed against skirt and cardigan
Like huge leaves fresh
From desire's diary,
Intimate reflections
Held up for appraisal

By her quizzical blonde head
Whose floral arrangement
Admires itself
As if picked already
From the warm bank

Of this glassy river
Where my own reflection
Hangs for a moment
With its basketful
Of wine and roses.

BLUE MOZART

after Dufy

Mozart framed
By so much blue
Is moony music
Calling you

To play me play me
As you please
While my distraction
Shall be these

Entanglements
Of leaf and bell
Which in their fashion
Love you well

Preferring
Secretive display
To such symphonic
Light of day

That only envy
Can be seen
In windows framing
Too much green

BRUSH-STROKES

The Child to the Painter

These snowflake ciphers
Of your brushwork, two
Last-minute smudges (dress
And bonnet
Thankyou sir) are me
Tugging my mother
(With our backs to you)
Towards a bay
Which is blue
Almost – well, a sort of
Dove-grey really
For the sake of your picture

Which is good, your picture,
(Well most of it) really
Except for that sort of
Not-quite-blue
You've made the bay
Which pleases you
No doubt sir (or my mother)
But to me
Like a lost bonnet
A spoiled dress
Seems adding two and two
And getting ciphers.

Poor Tree

It has (hasn't it?) an air
Of somehow not having been there
Yesterday, a hasty
Sudden bewilderment, wobbly

Like this poem, more than a shade
Rash in its sinuous red
Root of a trunk
(Don't you think?)

But urgent, in a rush,
Unabashed, its full blush
Saying *I got here*
With no time to spare

And like these words, provisional,
With no time at all
To be what they might, poor tree,
Though nevertheless meant lovingly.

The New Hat

Adjusting it,
Her confident hands
Already invite
A close-gloved wind's

Brow-pressure
Beneath the brim
Or intimate seizure
Of her dress's hem

As if to say
What common storm
Can offer me
The slightest harm?

And even the sun
Which seems no threat
Will have to reckon
With such a hat.

Entr'acte

The cuff-link whispers to the glove:
Such elegance, and all for love.

The glove confesses to the glass:
Oh how slowly five acts pass.

The glass is lifted to the eye:
Show me a tear I cannot dry.

The eye says nothing to the heart:
Such elegance, and all for art.

The Boathouse

A boat stole out
This early morning
And the doors hang open
Left behind

As love must always
Keep the whole day waiting
Dawn to dusk
Yet never mind.

AN AMATEUR WATER-COLOURIST TO
THOMAS GIRTIN

Your White House catches the post
From its numinous hinterland
To remind me, although I still boast
A watery brush in my hand,
That the world has gone penny-plain
Since I set out with so much hope
For those first strokes smudged by rain
On the back of an envelope.

EVERY LITTLE MOUSE

With impetuous recoil and jarring sound
The hatch heaved open like a huge suitcase
And Mickey masks clamped tight to every face
Packed Disneyland forever underground.

A siren played its silly symphony
While tearful Minnies waved a last farewell.
What was this hatch if not the gates of hell
And every little mouse a you or me?

Before the count went up to two or three
The hatch was down, the battens in their place.
A presidential Pluto'd proved that space
Was just what darkness cracked it up to be.

Some movies come a second time around
But this is one that surely never will.
Where every little mouse is who can tell?
No whiskered evidence has yet been found.

THE MAD PARROT'S COUNTDOWN

10   9   Wait (!)
Pieces of 8   pieces of 8
TERMINATE
7   6   Are you still alive
My hearties?   5
Gold rings   but listen I've
Learnt more
4
(Make Love not War)
3   2
It's down to you
Yo ho ho   Yo ho WHO (?)
1
Is 1
Is a bottle of rum
And ever more shall be so
Be so   be so
Be   ZERO . . .

THE CIRCUIT

Once more out of this shoe-box
(Christmas Accessories) dear tangled friends
With your plaited emerald flex
And familiar chime of chip-chink
Tumbling over my wrist, for the mind's
Ease for a moment I have you to thank

For my father's warm hand resting
Briefly on mine as again together
We number the dead ones and the wrong
Connections, restoring a light
Whose fitful flick and quiver
Is the love we shall celebrate

Tomorrow with the decked tree
Earthed in its yearly circuit
Of recurrence. When I say
Happy Christmas my own ghost
Will shine along the branches, lit
By all that is never lost

Though very soon forgotten. In two weeks
We shall be back here, dulled
And searching for this battered box I take
You from tonight to be, dear tangled friends,
A light of the world
Before the dark descends.

ON A LINE FROM PASTERNAK

Life is not a stroll across a field.
Whatever else it is it isn't that.
And luck is something more than the black cat
Which crossed your path just once when, still a child,
You thought there was no other beast in view –
That pussens sauntered by for none but you.

He didn't. Not a whisker left to chance
The necessary journey that he took
Out of his picture in your story book
To where your own son's wilful innocence
Finds and returns him, still beguiled
By life that seems a stroll across a field.

THE COST

Let this poem step
From its own perfection
And words be themselves again
In sweet disorder –
An undressed language,
A simple purpose
Like the child's tyrannical
Me! Me! Me!

But that little face
Is of deprivation,
A stone, a cloud
Or a flower, autonomous,
Plucking its petals
One by one.